BEST PRACTICES IN

DIGITAL
MEDIA

A BEGINNING DEVELOPER'S GUIDE
TO PROJECT ORGANIZATION AND
STRUCTURE

FIRST EDITION

BY TODD SHELTON

INDIANA UNIVERSITY –
PURDUE UNIVERSITY INDIANAPOLIS

cognella®
academic publishing

Bassim Hamadeh, CEO and Publisher
Michael Simpson, Vice President of Acquisitions
Jamie Giganti, Senior Managing Editor
Miguel Macias, Graphic Designer
Angel Schultz, Senior Field Acquisitions Editor
Michelle Piehl, Project Editor
Alexa Lucido, Licensing Coordinator
Allie Kiekofer, Interior Designer

First published in the United States of America in 2016 by Cognella, Inc.
Trademark Notice: Product or corporate names may be trademarks or registered trade-marks, and are used only for identification and explanation without intent to infringe.

Cover image copyright © 2013 Depositphotos/Kolett.
Interior images copyright © 2012 Depositphotos/bioraven.
copyright © 2011 Depositphotos/creatOR76.

Printed in the United States of America

ISBN: 978-1-63487-301-7(pbk) / 978-1-63487-302-4 (br)

cognella
academic publishing

www.cognella.com   800-200-3908

CONTENTS

This book is dedicated to my parents for being the best parents, and teaching me to never give up—*God bless both of them.*

ACKNOWLEDGMENTS

I will say that writing this book has been an experience, and I wouldn't have been able to complete this book without the support of several people in my personal and professional life, and I would like to take this time to thank them for the help and advice.

First is to Carrie Rector for proofreading the entire book more than a dozen times, and helping me correct a lot of the mistakes. She helped me stay on track and keep my thoughts straight, and for that I'm truly thankful.

To Dr. M. Pauline Baker for being a great mentor on my path through college, and showing me that programming is more than just sitting in a cubical.

The next two people I want to thank are Mathew A. Powers MFA and Zebulun M. Wood MS for the advice they gave me during the process of this book. Working with them is a great honor.

Finally, I would like to thank my sister for the help and support she gave me while writing this book. Thank you Teresa.

ABOUT THE AUTHOR

Todd Shelton is a lecturer at IUPUI's School of Informatics and Computing in Indianapolis, Indiana.

Todd spent his undergraduate and graduate years focusing on web and Flash development and physcial computing.

He used his knowledge to create interactive-media projects at a local award-winning design/development company and later used his expertise to work on more large-scale projects. He continues to use his expertise to do freelance projects for multiple clients.

Todd uses his industry knowledge to educate students on project processes along with essential design/development skills. He also educates the public on new development tools by running a successful user group called Dev Workshop which also hosts an annual conference for all things media. You can also find some of his tutorials on YouTube.

CHAPTER ONE

WHY SHOULD I READ THIS BOOK?

Are you new to project creation or to the digital media industry? Have you ever opened up a project folder and seen files scattered everywhere? Have you worked at a company and opened up some of their projects and couldn't understand how the project flowed?

If any of the above applies to you, then this book will help you understand why being organized is necessary in both your personal and professional careers. If you are going to do any kind of media development, then this book is a must-read.

There are a lot of books that talk about project and asset management, but few talk about the project creation itself. A well-organized and properly planned project will not only help you keep track of your files and media, it will help you collaborate on projects with your team.

Some people think that creating a well-structured project is easy—and for some professionals, it might be—but for others, it takes practice. After reading this book, you will notice half of the people in your work area and classroom create projects with files and folders scattered everywhere.

I will try to help you understand why it's so important to organize your project's folder structure and how staying organized will help you succeed in your career. I will explain techniques industry professionals use to keep their entire team up to date on their projects, which in turn speeds up project time lines and increases your client's respect for your company.

I am a programmer by trade, but I have worked on many projects that didn't involve programming of any kind. So, throughout this book, I will be discussing different project types to show how they all have the same structure. The only difference between professions, whether it be video, audio, 3-D, or Web, might be the differing industry nomenclature. For example, Web developers and IT professionals call their folders *directories*, whereas video professionals might prefer the term *bins*; they are still folders, and as such we will be using the term *folders* for the entirety of this book.

Although the folder structure described in this book is for larger projects, smaller projects can still benefit from similar, but scaled-down, structure. In either case, you should still practice good project creation habits whenever possible.

CHAPTER TWO

SCATTERBRAINED? WORK IT OUT!

After working in the industry for six years and teaching at various levels for the past five years, I have seen a lot of people creating projects. You can't imagine how unorganized people can be—even the ones you think are the most professional. There is nothing worse than being added to a work project and not being able to get your mind wrapped around their workflow. You start to think that whoever created these projects was scatterbrained. Well, I have been in that situation, and it is not a fun one to be involved in. That is the main reason behind this book: to help others avoid this.

It's time to get organized and eliminate this chaos!

Properly planning your project will help you create a sound and well-organized folder structure. I know that sounds so simple, but yet for some people, it can be really hard. So, let's talk about what I mean by properly planning your project.

You should never underestimate any project, from the simplest to the biggest, as they all have their challenges. I remember the first time my boss asked me to create an augmented reality project for our company Christmas card. I thought it was going to be a simple project, so I just jumped in and started programming.

The finished project ended up having animated 3-D models, multiple audio files, and a lot of images. Needless to say, I didn't plan properly, and at the end of the project, it took me an entire day to organize the project to be ready to archive. That project taught me a lot.

It's possible to work backward like I did, but it is not good practice; it will significantly decrease your project time. I'll talk more about this in Chapter 4, but now let's talk about planning your folder structure at the beginning of a task to create an organized project.

Let's look at my folder structure at the beginning of the project and then at its completion. This was supposed to be a simple project, so I started with a very simple folder structure:

Starting Project Structure

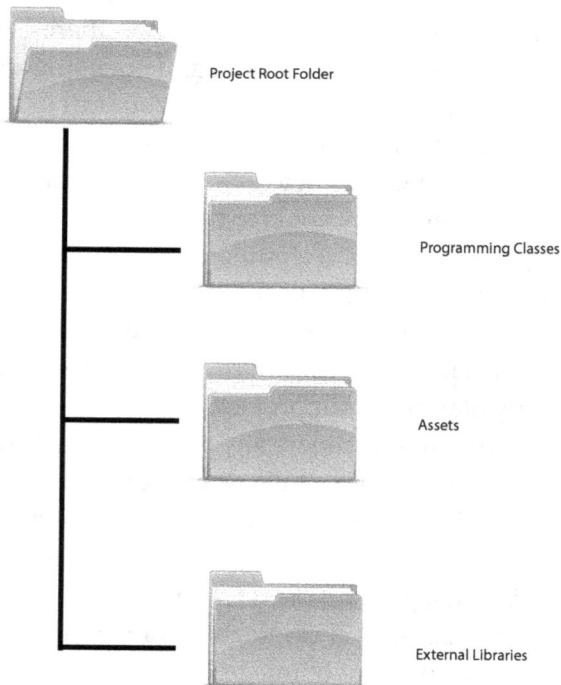

FIGURE 2.1. Image of simple project structure.

Now, let's take a look at the completed project:

Finished Project Structure

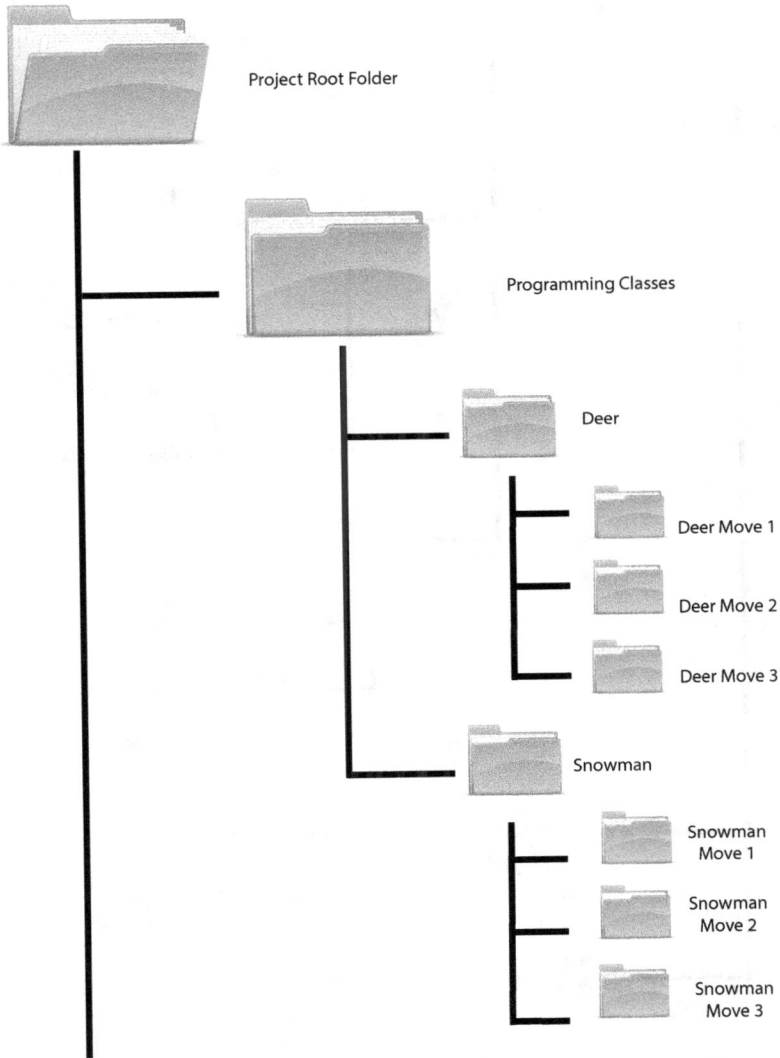

FIGURE 2.2. Image of finished folder structure.

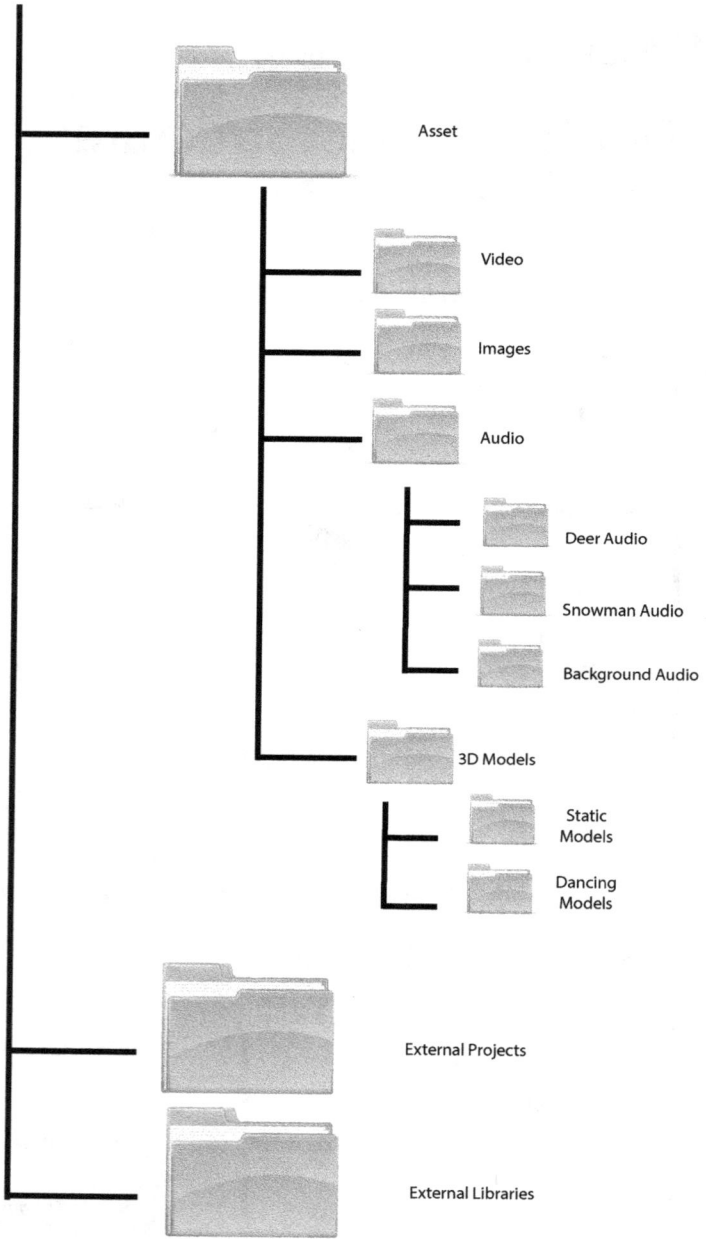

Asset

Video

Images

Audio

Deer Audio

Snowman Audio

Background Audio

3D Models

Static
Models

Dancing
Models

External Projects

External Libraries

FIGURE 2.3. Image of finished folder structure, bottom portion.

As you can see, it grew quite a bit during the course of the project; the project grew from three folders to 21 folders. Let's have a closer look at the folder structure at the beginning of the project. Imagine if these were the only folders I used. All of the programming classes—each Deer move and each Snowman move—were all combined into the *Classes* folder. As a result, it would take a long time to locate the Deer move 3 programming classes. The same can be said for the *Assets* folder. All the video, images, audio, and 3-D models would all be in the same folder. Imagine the amount of files that would be in that folder; it would take forever to find a specific file you were looking for! Well, maybe not forever, but it would take a lot of time—time you don't have to complete the project.

You can see why proper planning is so important. This becomes even clearer when multiple developers or designers work on a project. Having all the different asset types in one large folder would probably infuriate your coworkers and add unnecessary wasted time to the project.

So, how can I stop being scatterbrained and get my projects on track?

Whether you are a team of one or a team of many, it is good to lay out your folder structure at the very beginning of your project, before any files are added to the task. To this day, I still find this step hard to do because I want to jump right in and start setting things up, but that is where project creation goes wrong.

To plan your project properly from the beginning, grab an old-fashioned pencil and paper or a more modern whiteboard, and start laying out your project. Post-it notes are also a good way to represent folders to determine folder structures. Some prefer to use text documents and nested lists to illustrate the folder structure. With these simple tools, you can quickly and easily make changes to the architecture of your project.

Next, you need to decide what folders to include. Think of the entire project and the many assets it will take to complete the project; make a folder for each category. Be as specific and detailed as possible. Here is an example of a simple video project using a text document.

Client John Doe Video Project Planning Document

Project Root Folder (clientName followed by project name)
- *project docs (location of all documents for this project)*
- *sfx (video, sfx footage)*
- *audio (audio files)*
- *sequences (video sequences)*
- *bRoll (b-roll video)*
- *interview (client interviews)*
- *graphics*
- *lower-thirds (lower thirds)*

Here is a look at the whiteboard example:

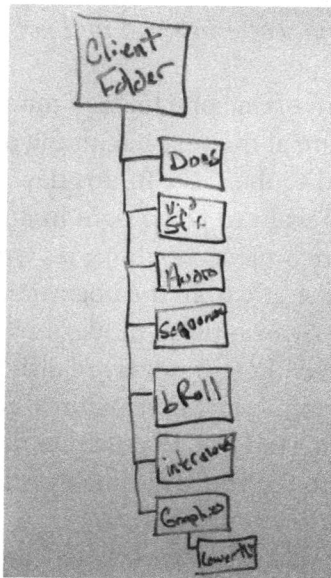

FIGURE 2.4. Image of whiteboard.

This is a very simple example, but notice I try to cover most assets/files that will be used. It is also very important to write a description for each folder. I know this might sound like overkill, but when you are writing or typing words, you rationalize what you are writing. This might make you realize that you need a client logos folder in the *Graphics* folder rather than just lower thirds or the fact that we don't have a scripts folder for this project.

Some people might just use one folder called *Graphics* and store every asset they are going to use in that folder. I have done this before, and it can get really chaotic when mixing all different types of graphics for a project. During a project, you will most likely have logos, still images, lower thirds, and many other types. You will need to keep them organized to make them easier to find.

After you have created a multitude of projects, you will begin to simplify this process because you will start seeing how projects are formed and grow. You might come up with better ways to approach project planning, but while you are learning, keep creating projects like this—it will help you stay organized. Some studios have one person create the default project structure, and then the senior editors or developers finish the rest of the project setup. This makes sense for those companies and ensures a strict folder structure.

Let's move on to the project structure and how to set one up.

CHAPTER THREE

WHY USE A PROJECT STRUCTURE?

Some very naive people might wonder why we have to have such a strict folder structure, and if you have ever looked at their projects, you will understand why they ask that question.

Once you create a good default folder structure, everything else just falls into place. The moons align, harmony happens in the workplace, and your projects start getting done faster.

Like I mentioned in the last chapter, there are some project managers who create the initial project folder structure. The developers then build from this initial structure during project creation. This ensures that all projects have the same project folder structures, regardless of the media.

To begin your project, there will always be a project root folder. Without this folder, chaos sets in and projects begin to break. The folder is called the root folder because it is the foundation for your entire project, similar to the roots of a tree. Nothing should be located outside of this project folder. Images, project documents, videos, Web files, models ... basically, anything that will help create the project must be inside this root folder. This folder should be named accordingly, as well. For instance, do not name it *Project Root Folder* like I did in the following image. The naming convention of this folder should make sense to the project. For instance, naming the folder

ABCCorp _Soap Commercial_2015 is descriptive of the project and will make it easier to locate the folder later in the archives. Do not name it something generic, as you will notice in the image below.

Project Root Folder

FIGURE 3.1. Image of root folder.

Now that we have a good understanding of the root folder, let's talk about what needs to be inside this folder.

Inside the root folder, we have other folders that set up the overall structure of your project. The naming of these folders will vary by project, but there should be a couple of default folders. For example, some common folders could be a *Project Document* folder and a *Text Content* folder:

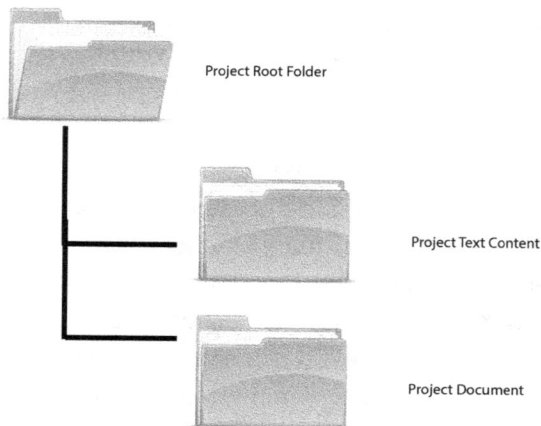

Project Root Folder

Project Text Content

Project Document

FIGURE 3.2. Example of common folders.

As you will notice with the image above, there are only a couple of folders, but these folders will exist in every project we create and hold some of the most important data for our project. Now it's time to talk about the content of these folders.

The *Project Text Content* folder contains all the text (or *copy*, as some call it) for the entire project. This folder could have subfolders if there are enough files to further categorize. For instance, maybe we are creating a mobile or Web application for a client and they have given us all the copy for the application. This is a good time to organize the project copy so other team members on the project can easily find the correct text to put in the application.

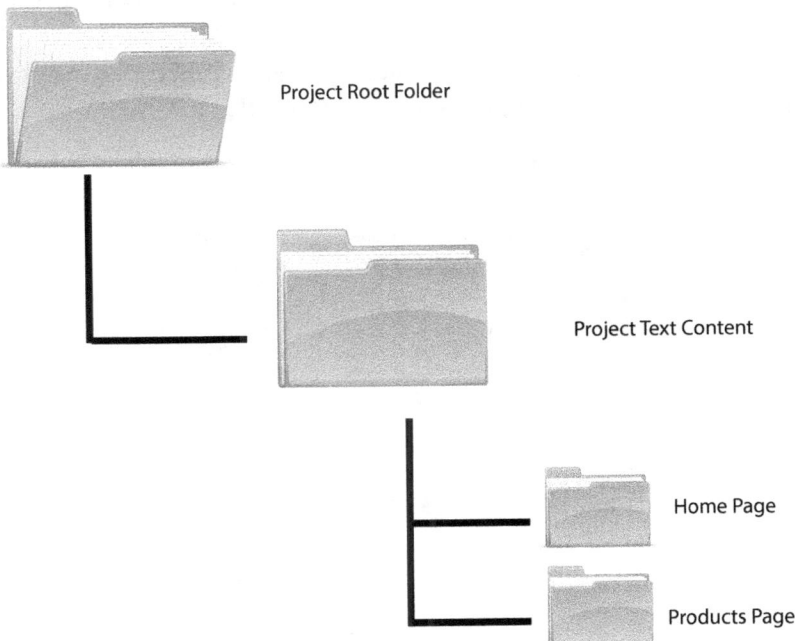

Project Root Folder

Project Text Content

Home Page

Products Page

FIGURE 3.3. Organized text content.

Let us focus now on the *Project Document* folder. This folder contains all the information about the project. It will have project dimensions, colors, font families, and any other information that you need to create the project. This is one of the most important folders you will create. It could hold one long Word document or several. Either way, it needs to be updated anytime the project details change.

In these examples, I have given the folders what I thought were appropriate names. However, you might want to name your folders something different. Whatever you name the folders, make sure you name them something that makes sense to your company and your company's workflow. Depending on the nature of the project, however, your naming conventions might need to change. Don't tie yourself down to a certain naming convention. Choose folder names that make sense to the organization of the particular media project. Regardless of what you choose, you should keep them consistent within the particular medium.

Here is an example of an audio project. Notice that we have similar folders, but they are named differently.

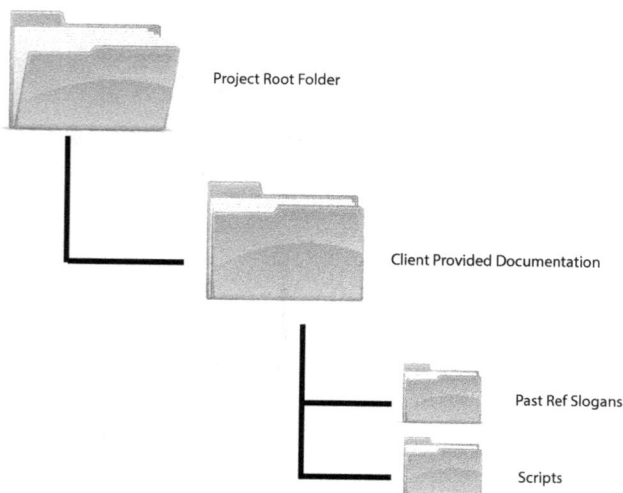

Project Root Folder

Client Provided Documentation

Past Ref Slogans

Scripts

FIGURE 3.4. Audio project structure.

These folders contain files provided by the client. These files might come in handy for reference or for a place to get sound bites.

Now that we have a good understanding of the default folder structure, we'll take a look at how we can expand our folders to allow more members to work on this project simultaneously.

In this next example, we will look at a sample game project. Most people don't understand what it takes to create a video game, but if we break it down and look at the individual parts, I think you will see how big this project could grow and how we can use our project structure to allow multiple team members to work together.

I have never worked on a console video game before, but I have friends who do, and they say that there are up to 50 to 100 people working on a game at one time. Now, imagine how big these projects can get. Without proper project organization, your game can get out of control.

In this scenario, we are going to have 30 developers and designers working on our game at one time. We need to have a way for all of them to stay organized and share files with each other (and not mess up anyone else's projects).

First things first: you need to come up with a basic folder structure that will allow all of our developers to work together without interfering with each other.

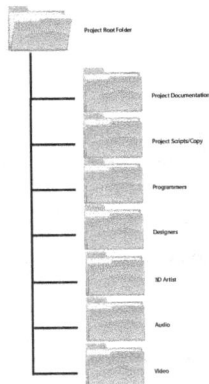

FIGURE 3.5. Sample game project.

Notice the project structure begins with our default folders. The *Project Documentation* folder holds all the project information, and the *Project Scripts/Copy* folder holds all the projects' scripts for the characters and any text that needs to be added to the screens.

Next, we have five folders designated for the different development teams that will be working on this game. First off, we have the *Programmers* folder. This folder will be designated for the programmers only, and *only* the programming team will create any subfolders that need to be made.

The next folder we will look at is one of the most important folders in this entire game project: the *Designers* folder. Why is it so important? Because it holds all the graphics needed for the entire game. This folder will end up connecting to the *Programmers* folder, the *3-D Artist* folder, and the *Video* folder. It is very important that once the subfolders are created for this project folder they do not change.

One way this might look is shown in the next image. Notice that we are being very specific on how we name these folders and their subfolders.

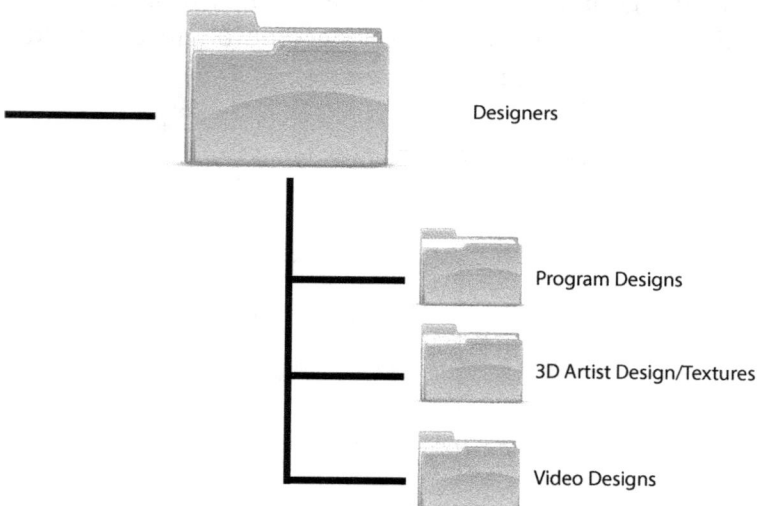

Designers

Program Designs

3D Artist Design/Textures

Video Designs

FIGURE 3.6. Naming folders.

Once you get these folders named, you should *not* rename them. Renaming these folders can cause the entire project to break, and this is where some people don't understand the reason why they can't just rename these when they want. Let me explain why.

Let's say that you are a 3-D artist and you are using a texture in one of your models. To find this texture, you would navigate to the *Designers* folder > *3-D Artist Design/Textures* folder, and find the texture file that you need.

Now that you have this file imported into your project, your software remembers the path back to the folder where the file is stored. However, if somebody renames that folder within the *Designers* folder, it will break the link between the folders. These paths are covered more extensively in the next chapter, but for now, just understand that you cannot rename folders without breaking the file paths.

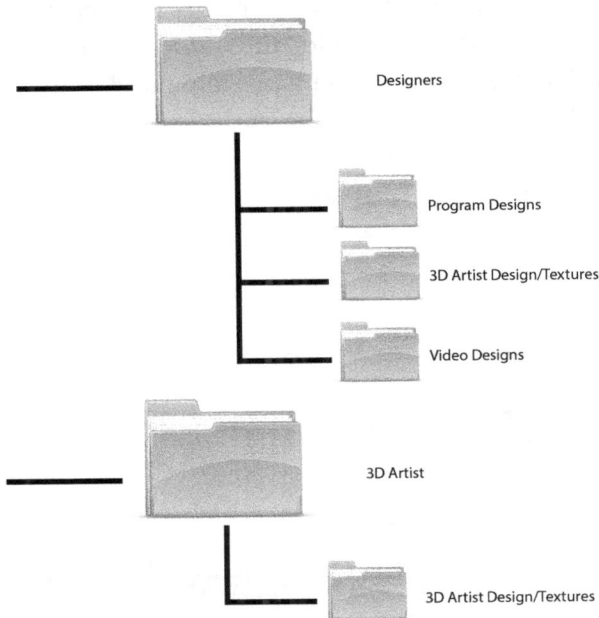

Designers

Program Designs

3D Artist Design/Textures

Video Designs

3D Artist

3D Artist Design/Textures

FIGURE 3.7. Linking File Between Folders

Broken Link:

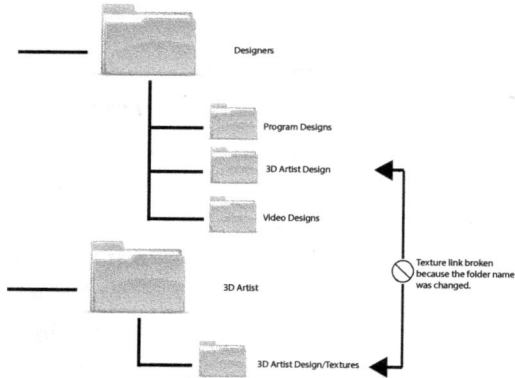

FIGURE 3.8. Broken link due to the renaming of the folder.

The second most important folder in this project is the *Audio* folder. Just like the *Designer* folder, the *Audio* folder will also connect to the *Programmers* and the *Video* folders.

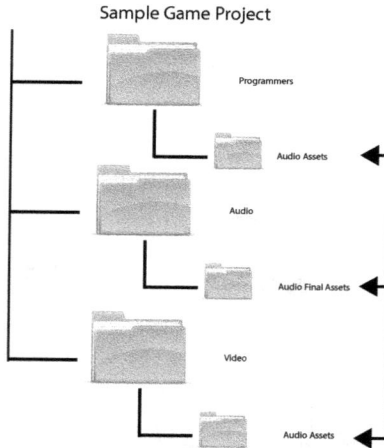

FIGURE 3.9. Audio folder connection to other folders.

Again, you cannot rename folders, or that link will be broken as well. I know I keep saying not to rename the folders, but it is very important. A senior team member should decide whether to make any changes to the folder names.

We haven't even started developing the game, but you can see how our folder structure is growing. The main objective is to keep your project organized and structured. Because of the strict folder structure, you can scale the project bigger without affecting other team members. This is very important, as we do not want to break the project.

Let's continue on with the rest of the folders in this project. I have mentioned the two folders that I think are the most important, but that does not mean the rest aren't necessary. So, let's talk about the *Video* folder. The programmers will use the videos stored within the *Programmers Video* folder to incorporate into the game. Therefore, another connection is made between project folders.

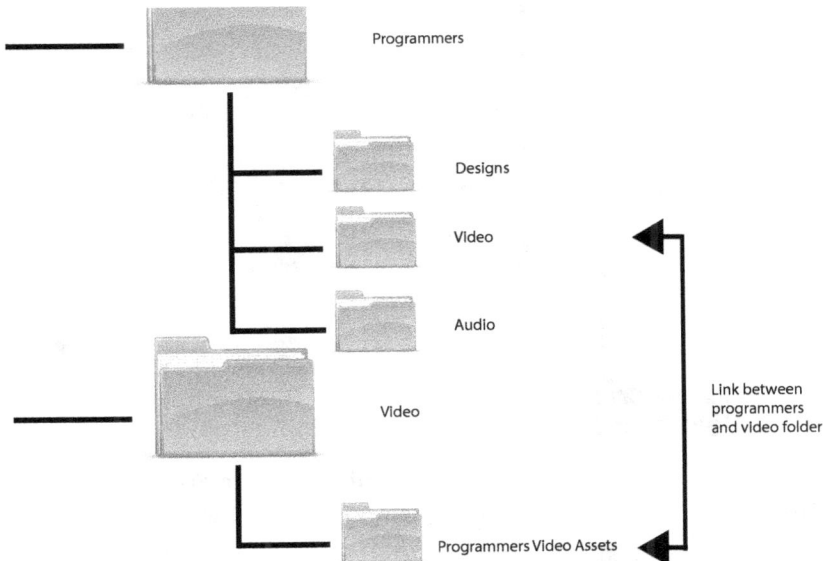

FIGURE 3.10. Linking *Programmers* video folder to *Video*.

So far, we have been looking at the *connection* between the folders. Now, we will examine individual folders. The first one we will start with is the *Video* folder. This folder can often be the hardest to organize because of the sheer number of video files and audio files; it is often massive.

For this reason, organization is even more important.

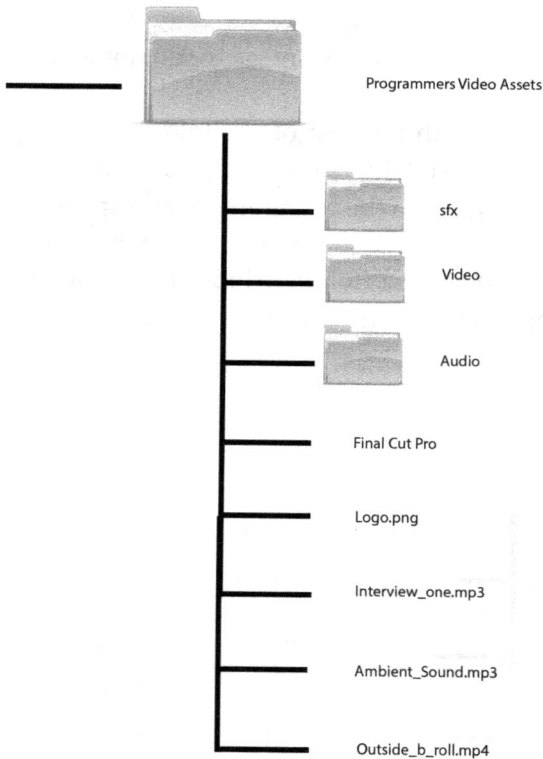

FIGURE 3.11. Files in root folder that need to be organized.

As you can see from the example above, there are a few files in the root folder that must be organized. Notice how there are only three folders in this project: *Audio, Video,* and *sfx.* There should probably be a lot more—one for graphics, for instance, lower thirds, B-roll, and any other folders that would keep your projects organized. This is a simple example, but disorganization can get out of hand when a project gets bigger. So, let's look at what our game video folder should look like.

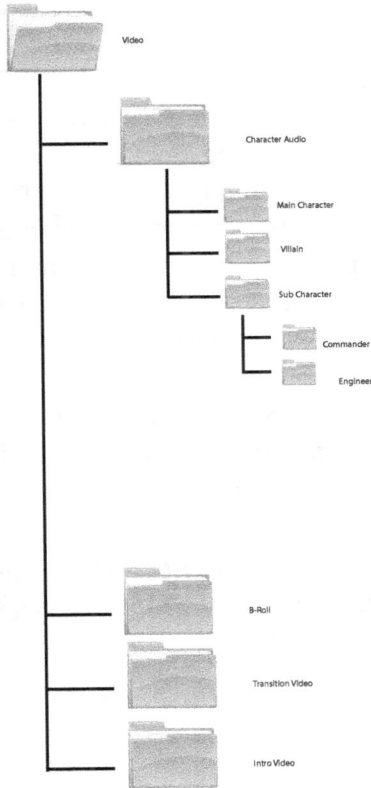

FIGURE 3.12. Video folder organized.

As you can see, new folders and subfolders are added to the main *Video* folder. The names of these folders should be very descriptive, so other team members know what they mean without question. In this example, our *Character Video* folder contains three subfolders and two subfolders within the *Sub Characters* folder. These videos will be used for transition videos to different parts of the game. That is why each character needs its own folder.

We could continue to make examples of how to structure your folders in this video game example, but I hope you're understanding how it's starting to fit together. A project of this size could have hundreds of folders, and if you do not take the time to stay organized, you and your team could easily fall behind.

Now that we have taken a look at how to set up folders and subfolders, let's take a look at the file paths that connect all of these files and folders within a project.

NOTE: It is important to know that throughout this book the folder names and some file names have spaces in them. This is done for readability. This is not good practice. You should not leave spaces when naming folders or files. Either use *a* - or *an* _ between words. You can also use camelCase. Notice the letter of the second word is capitalized. By adding spaces, you will affect the way the path to the file works.

CHAPTER FOUR

UNDERSTANDING PATHS (AND I DON'T MEAN THE HIKING KIND)

Before we even begin this chapter, let me begin by saying I know there are more than two operating systems out there, but for the sake of this book, we will stick with Windows and Macs.

This chapter will stress the importance of organizing your files, folders, and your project as a whole. We also will take a more in-depth look at why we cannot rename the files and folders after the project creation without having some issues with file linkage.

One of the hardest things for individuals to understand is the path to the files and folders. Regardless of your project's purpose—video, 3-D, or Web development, (especially web development)—you need to understand why you cannot just move your files and folders and expect your project to run smoothly. This is why it's important to understand the difference between absolute and relative paths.

Most software will not show you the path to files and folders, unless you really look for it. It just holds them in memory and keeps track of them using an absolute path. It is called an absolute path because it starts at the root of the operating system and lists every folder until it finds the file you want. If any of these folder names or drive letters change, the link that was saved in your project is now broken.

Below you can see an example of an absolute path for a PC and a Mac.

PC:

C:\USER\Documents\project_name\filename.doc

Mac:

/Users/yourname/Documents/project_name/filename.doc

Notice that the PC version starts with the drive letter. In most cases, the drive letter is "C." The Mac side starts a little differently from the PC: it starts with the user folder, which is basically like the drive letter on a PC. Either way, both start at the root of your operating system's hard drive, working its way through the folders to find the file you want. Notice the direction the slashes are going. The PC uses a backslash (\ ), and the Mac employs a forward slash (/). It is important to know which way the slashes lean in case you ever need to fix a path that is broken.

Now, there is one other absolute path I want to mention, and you might use this if you are pulling your assets from a website. If your project needs to do this, then you will see an absolute path that looks like the following link:

http://www.domain.com/project_folder/file.jpg

It looks like a Web address and it is an absolute path, but instead of a drive letter or a user folder, it uses the http and domain name as its root, and then steps through the Web directories or folders to the file you need. Again, you can't change the name of any of the folders, or this link will be broken.

Another place you might see an absolute path is when you are importing files from a server. The path for importing files from a server would look something like the examples below:

Mac:

smb://company.org/file-share/music_library

PC:

file:////company.org/file-share/music_library

Again, if you change any folder on the server, the path is broken. Do not rename or move folders.

Most people will never see the path to a file unless you are a Web developer, but either way, it is important you know what absolute links are and how they work. This is why many people do not understand why their projects break when they move files around.

Let's take a look at a video project now.

Your company has a lot of special effects footage and audio in a folder on a server or hard drive. You open up the media browser and pull the files into the project, making an absolute path to that file within your project. Your project will store this path in its project memory, making a connection to the file on the server. Let's look at the example, remembering the file isn't really in your project—it is just linked to the file stored on the server.

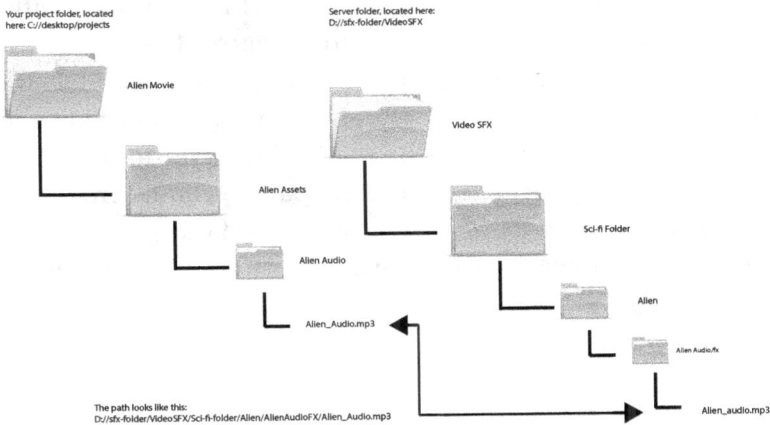

FIGURE 4.1. Link to a remote audio file on server.

Someone moves the server folder to another drive, which now changes the file path from this:

D://sfx-folder/VideoSFX/Sci-fi-folder/Alien/AlienAudioFX/ AlienAudio.mp3

to this:

E://sfx-folder/VideoSFX/Sci-fi-folder/Alien/AlienAudioFX/ AlienAudio.mp3

Your project's path to the audio file is now broken, because it still thinks it is located in the D:// drive. Chances are your software will ask you to relink the media, but sometimes it may not, and you will have to search for the files.

Some of today's software will copy the file from the server and store it within the projects folder structure. ProTools, an audio program, does a very good job of copying the files from a remote server or hard drive and storing them within your project, saving you the hassle of dealing with broken links. Unlike the examples above that use absolute links, software programs like ProTools use relative links to link to files.

Relative links are links that are created based on their relative location to the file you are working on. Relative links are used within a project to link to other files and are the preferred link to use. Now, we'll examine another example to demonstrate this type of path.

Our Web developer needs to link to an image located in the image folder. Rather than using an absolute path to link to the image, the developer can use a relative path to connect to the file. By using a relative path, you can ensure that if this project moves to another computer or hard drive, the link to the file stays intact.

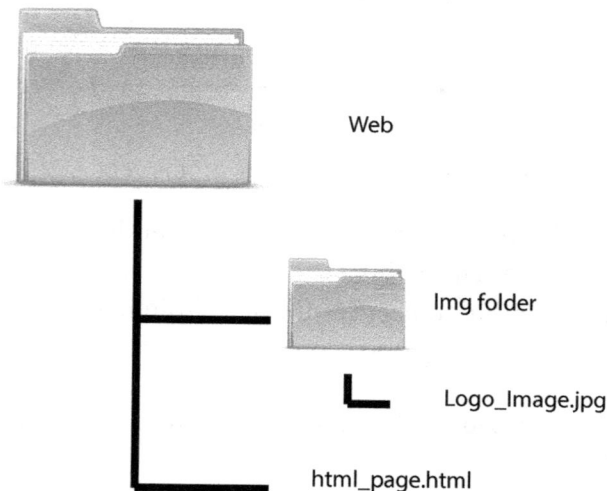

FIGURE 4.2. Showing image file location compared to html_page.html file.

Using the illustration above, the relative path to Logo_Image.jpg from our html_page.html would look like this:

Img-folder/logo_Image.jpg.

Notice that there are no drive letters or folders that start with *user* like a Mac. It is just a straight path to the file from within your project. Since *html_page.html* is at the same level as the *Img_folder*, we can just call the folder by name and then use the forward slash to move within the folder to the image file. But what happens if the files are not on the same level? How do you write the path then?

If you really want to understand paths and how they work, look at some UNIX examples. They will show you a great way to maneuver through your computer's folders, but who wants to read about UNIX when we are concerned with our media projects?

There are a few ways to get to a file or folder if they are not on the same level. The location of this file or folder relative to the file you are working on determines how the path is written. Look at

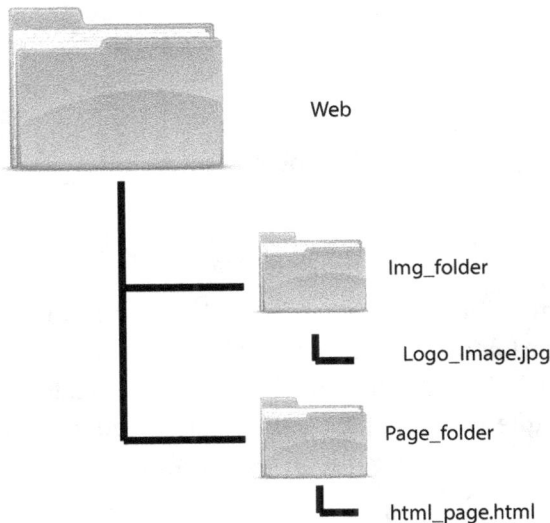

FIGURE 4.3. Showing image file location to new html file location.

the example below. You need to link the image *Logo_Image.jpg* to your working file, *html_page.html*.

In the example above, in order for the html file to access the image, you have to back out of the *SubPages folder*. You do this by creating a relative path like this:

../Img_folder/Logo_Image.jpg

The two periods (. .) will back out of the folder you are currently in. By using the (..), you are now in the WWW folder. Now, by adding the forward slash (/), you are ready to select the next folder:

../

In this example, we would want to put *Img_folder* after the /, . . /Img_folder   now we are in the *Img_folder*.

Then, we write the path the same way as before:

..	/	Img_folder	/	Logo_Image.jpg
backs out	moves into folder	folder name	moves into folder	file name

. . /Img_folder/logoImage.jpg

Now, no matter where you move the Web folder, as long as you do not rename the folders or files, all of the files will stay linked using that relative path. You could copy this folder and hand it to as many people as you wanted and the files will remain linked together.

There's another way to back out of folders, and that is to use one period (.) and a forward slash (/).

. / moves to the root folder.

If we added on to our project above and had several subfolders inside of our *SubPages* folder, then the quickest way to get to the Web folder is to put the (. / .). This way, you would move directly to the root folder, and your path would look like this:

./Img_folder/Logo_Image.jpg

You may be asking yourself why we don't do this all the time. That is because sometimes you do not need to go to the root folder; you may only have to move up one folder.

So, a final note on paths: If you have the option to make a relative path, I strongly recommend doing so.

CHAPTER FIVE

WHY ORGANIZING CAN HELP YOUR PROJECT RUN SMOOTHER

Thus far, you have learned how to organize your projects and why they need to be so strictly structured. You have also learned how to navigate around projects using absolute and relative paths, but absolute and relative paths have been around forever. Let's talk about something new and more exciting. We live in a world of technology, so we'll explore what you can do with your newfound knowledge on proper project structure.

When I first started in the industry, I was saving projects and keeping them around for future reference. There were limited storage options at the time, so I began storing files on old 3-½" floppy disks, then on CDs, and finally more modern USB drives. As technology progresses, so do the storage options for our information and project files.

Versioning control systems such as Git and SVN are some of the new advancements. These tools keep track of all the changes you make to your files and/or folders. If you're familiar with the popular tool Dropbox (another versioning control system tool), you might have noticed they keep track of different versions of your files; Git does the same thing. With these tools, you can go back and download the last version you saved. This is helpful if you need to revert to an older version because of programming errors, file corruption, or project changes. These versioning control tools help projects proceed smoother and keep everything organized. If you don't know about Git or SVN, it is definitely worth your time to investigate these options.

Currently, Git is the most popular versioning control system used by developers today, so I will discuss this tool. SVN is another such version control system (VCS) that is often used, especially in big corporations, but it works in a slightly different way.

As mentioned earlier, Git keeps track of all the changes you make to your files and folders like Dropbox. Say, for example, you have written a term paper and saved it in Dropbox. You have been editing the file for a while, when you realize you messed up the entire paper. Now, with these tools, you can go back and download the last version you saved, saving you time and trouble rewriting your entire paper. Although Dropbox is a more simplistic versioning control tool than Git or SVN, all of these tools work in this same way.

Versioning tools allow you to *push* changes that you have made to your project to a server. When you push changes, you essentially are uploading a version of your file to the server. This saves all your changes in a safe place. You can also *pull* all changes to your project from the server. When you pull changes, you simply download the files to your local computer and the tool adds the files to your local computer or updates the files if you have downloaded them previously to your machine. This is important if someone else has made changes to your project by making a pull from the server and updating your project. Now, you will have any and all changes made to the file, regardless of who made the changes. Do keep in mind, however, that these are simply versions of the original file. If you need to go back to the original document, it is still intact in the versioning tool.

Every file version takes up some memory on your server or local computer. Some companies don't offer unlimited versioning; they often limit the number of versions per file. Make sure you investigate the versioning restrictions of each tool before deciding on a VCS service.

These tools are widely used by many programmers and make it easy for larger programming teams to keep coding files current. The tools will also show conflicts in a file. For instance, let's say you and another programmer are working on the same file, not project, but *file*. These tools will show you the difference between your file and the other programmer's file. It will show you each line of code and what was added or deleted, not to mention the user who updated the file.

If you are an aspiring programmer, chances are you have worked by yourself on projects and not on a team. The aforementioned example happens frequently in projects, and you need to become familiar with merging files and working with a team on projects.

Although versioning control systems like Git and SVN are primarily used by programmers, other professionals in the media world can also benefit from using these tools. Programmers often take advantage of versioning due to the often complex nature of their work and numerous coding files. Media professionals such as video and audio developers and designers can use these tools just as effectively for their many files as well. Many studios use these tools to offer a greater collaborative environment that supports versioning control to create well-organized projects.

Some studios use these new technologies to keep their teams up to date on all of their projects' assets. Let's explore an example that illustrates this point. Susie and Billy have been teamed up to create a website for a client. After the creative process is done and their team is ready to dive into programming, the designer starts working on the overall layout and design of the website. If there has been a wireframe developed, the developer starts laying out the project and prepares to insert the assets generated by the designer.

Depending on the company you work for, it might vary on who generates the assets for the projects. On projects that are very code heavy, designers generally generate the assets. On small projects, sometimes the designers create the designs and hand the files off to the developers to do the asset generation, but in this case, Billy, the designer, will be creating the assets.

The project manager for this project has set up a default folder structure:

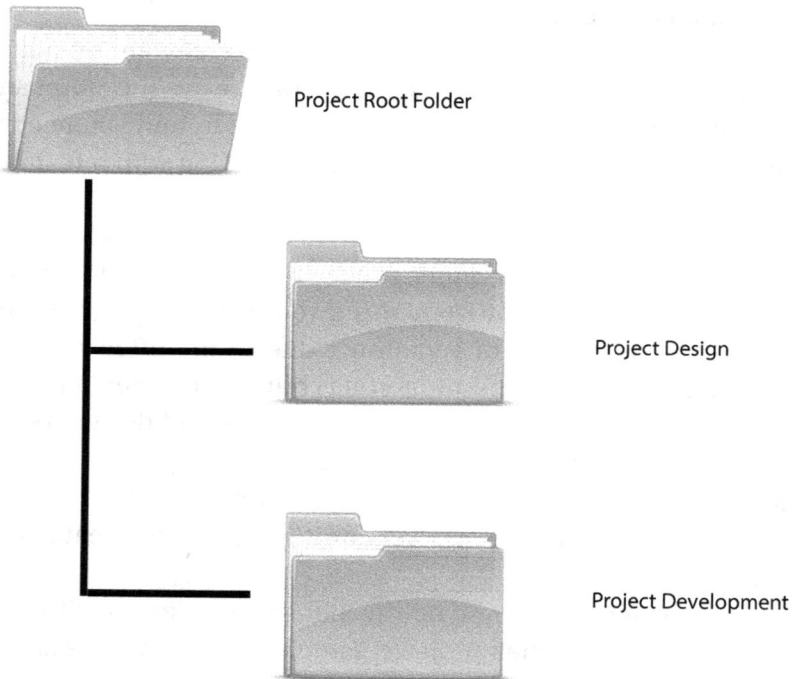

Project Root Folder

Project Design

Project Development

FIGURE 5.1. Project manager default folder structure.

Billy and Susie are added to this project as team members. Billy is the designer on this project and therefore stores all of his files and assets in a folder called *Project Design*. As Billy generates the image assets needed for the website, he stores them in subfolders located inside of the site assets folder. Notice below that Billy creates a site assets folder inside of Susie's development folder, as illustrated in the next image. Billy also creates folders called *background images, content images,* and *corporate logo.*

Billy creates those folders inside of Susie's development folder because most Web projects need one root folder. In this case, it is Susie's *development* folder. Having one root folder makes it easier for Susie to move it to the server when publishing the website.

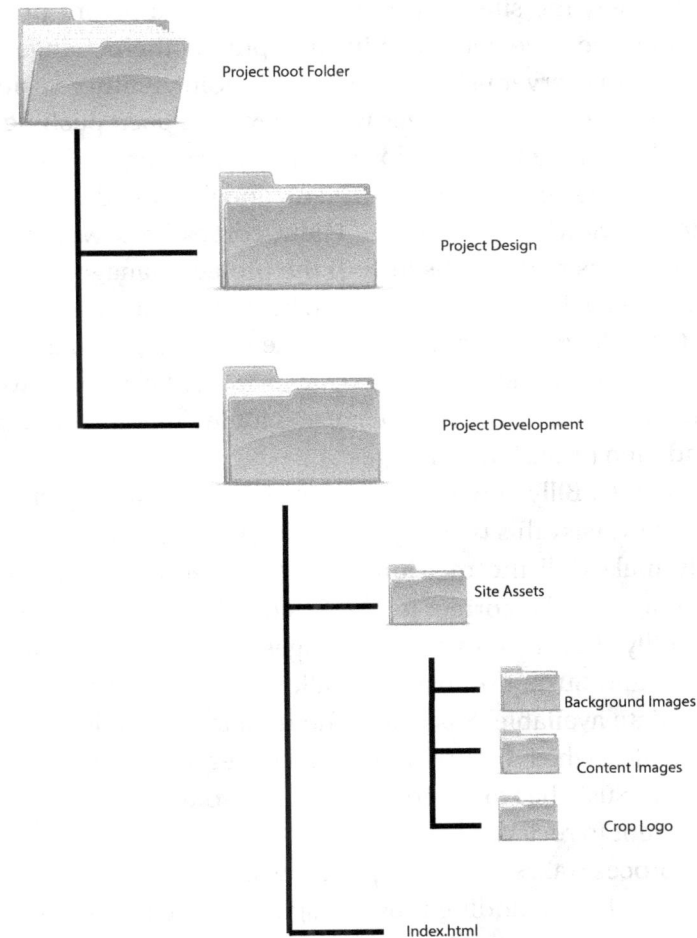

Project Root Folder

Project Design

Project Development

Site Assets

Background Images

Content Images

Crop Logo

Index.html

FIGURE 5.2. Susie's local folder structure.

Billy finally finishes generating all of the assets for the website and communicates to Susie that he is done with the assets and she can start adding those assets to the site. All of the images that Susie places on the webpage will be from the folders Billy created and stored inside of the *Site Assets* folder. Susie will use relative paths to link to the images on the website.

Susie has been working really hard and is ready to have the client preview the site. During this entire development process, Billy and Susie have been pushing and pulling their changes and updates to the server using Git. Up to this point, neither Susie nor Billy have noticed any changes while they have been pushing and pulling their project, but we do know that since they are using Git, their entire project has been backed up and versioned.

After previewing the site, the client comes back with several image changes to the website, and the project manager communicates to Billy these changes need to be done right away. Without using Git, Billy would have had to make the changes to all of the images and send those images back to Susie. Susie then would have to put those images in the correct folder, updating her project, and then publish the changes.

Thankfully, Billy and Susie are using Git for their project. Let's find out how easy this is going to be using this VCS tool.

Billy makes all the revisions the client requested and saves those images in the correct folders inside of Susie's development folder. Billy then pushes those changes to the server. The tools that Billy and Susie use inside Git allow them to see when there is an update available. Susie sees the update and pulls down the updated files, which in turn updates all of her images inside of her folders. All Susie has to do now is push that folder up to the server for the client to review.

This process takes out the step of Billy having to pass the images to Susie, and Susie adding those images to the correct folders so she can publish the site. They purposefully structured their folders so Billy can make changes to any of the images at any time during the project development, and Susie can automatically update her files once she pulls down those image updates. This is really nice compared to other studios' workflows.

Now, this is a very small project with only two people working on it. Imagine a project that has 30 to 40 people creating and revising assets all the time. This process allows files to be updated automatically; it saves time in the long run on people updating files in the final publishing folder.

The process I described can be used in any project: video, audio, motion graphics, or Web (like the example above). But I'm going to show another example with a different type of media to show how useful and versatile these versioning control system tools can be for any project development.

This next example involves a motion graphics project consisting of 3-D models, graphics, audio, video, and Web files. All of these files will be used to produce the motion graphics video. The Web portion will be used to display the video on a Web page when it's completed.

As you can guess, this project will be very large. The numerous files will have to be organized into several folders inside the main project folder. The end product for this project will be a Web page, so the developer will be in charge of publishing the folder for the end product.

Like all the previous examples, the project manager has structured our default project folder structure.

As you can see from the example above, the project manager has set up a folder for each piece of our project, including the *Project Publishing Web* folder, where all of our finished assets will be stored.

This project is a more advanced example because of all the intertwining folders. Let us examine how they all work together.

All of the project folders have subfolders for development, but when the developers and designers create their finalized assets, they will save those files in the appropriate project folder. For instance, the audio portion of the project will have its own

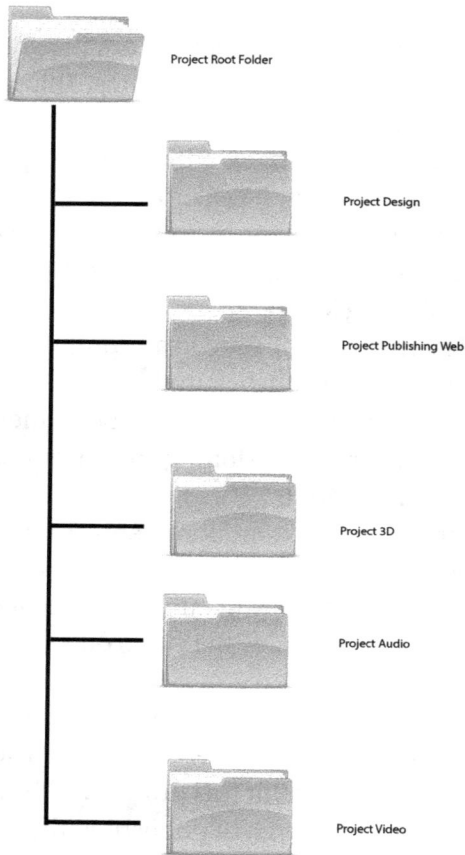

FIGURE 5.3. Motion graphics folder structure.

development process. The audio developers will work from the *Project Audio* folder and all of its subfolders to create their final audio file. This *Project Audio* folder will contain all the resource files that will become part of the audio files used in the project. When the final audio files are created, they will save the final files into the *Audio Assets* folder inside the *Video Project* folder to be used by the videographer. This is because these finished files now become the resource files the videographer will use to create the final video project that will be used in this project.

This setup works really well because if any tweaks need to be made to the audio file, they can edit the file, and it will be automatically updated in the video project by doing a pull from the server using Git.

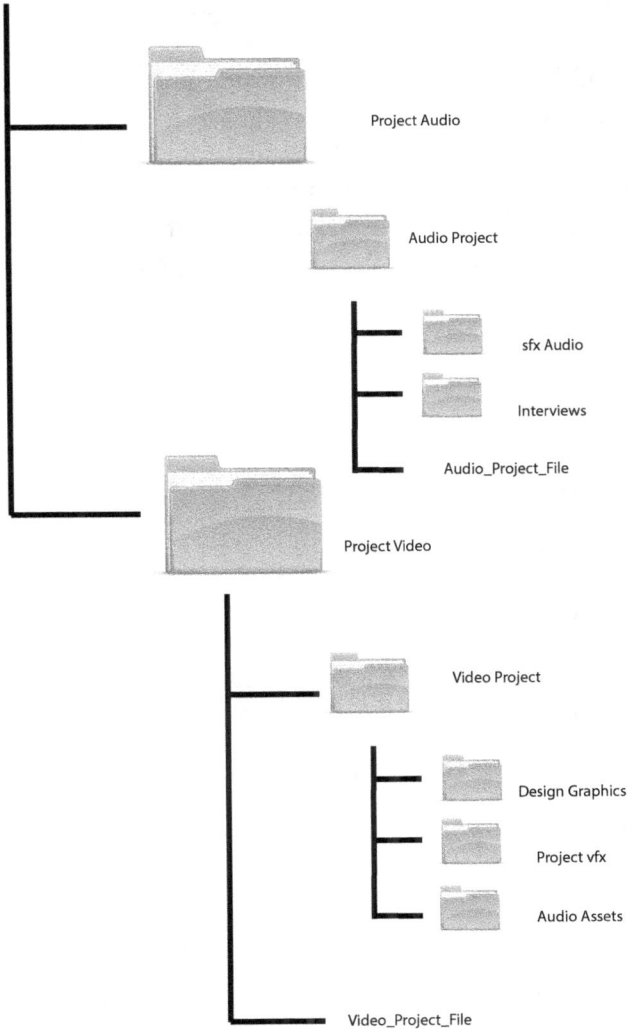

FIGURE 5.4. Storing files in another folder for ease of use.

This project structure will only work effectively if there is constant communication among the project's team members for the length of the video and audio files (in this example), but this should be built into any project process.

It is important to know each person on the team has this entire project folder on his or her local machine. That is how they update the other folders and push those changes to the server. All team members should be instructed not to touch any project folders other than their own.

Let's examine how the graphics team will interact with all of the folders in the project. The graphics team creates graphics for all areas of the project *except* for audio. Therefore, the only folder the graphics team will *not* touch is the audio folder. As you can see in

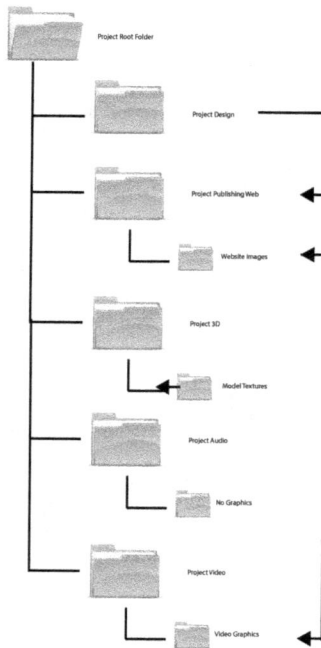

FIGURE 5.5. Graphics team connecting to all project folders.

the image below, the graphics team is a very important element to this project.

Typically, graphics are updated several times during the life cycle of a project. When the video team communicates to the graphics team that there is a graphics correction needed, the graphics team can make the changes and update the graphic file. Because the team is using Git for their collaboration, the files will update automatically, thereby updating the rest of the project for the other team members.

The same process would work for the Web and 3-D teams. In many cases, the developers on each team do not need to do anything to their project to switch out the images. They are automatically updated, since all of the images and graphics are connected through relative paths.

We could examine this process further to illustrate how all of these folders connect, but the concept is the same; you should begin to see how everything fits together to create a very organized project structure and working process. This example also illustrates how important and useful new technology can be for any project.

Versioning control systems like Git might not be the answer to all project processes, but it does help with efficiency. Many times, studios or production companies become complacent with project processes and structure and never look at new technology that might enhance their current system. While I can't say I blame them sometimes, it does take time to learn new ways to do things. However, in the end, keeping up with technology will only help your projects and your company run smoother.

CHAPTER SIX

I AM A <INSERT PERSON'S TITLE>, AND I DON'T NEED TO DO THIS

Although this book is mainly geared toward the digital media field, there are so many other creative fields that could benefit from this structure setup, thereby leading to better organization and streamlining the creative process.

If you are a media developer or designer, the advantages of proper project structure and process are clearly evident from the previous chapters and examples. These benefits can also be valuable for managers and directors. Ensuring the team operates as efficiently as possible is the main goal for management and directors, and this eases the entire process. Even though your current processes might work well, it is also important to continually look for improvements. Even owners can benefit in this structure by leading by example—showing the team that they adhere to the structure set forth and emphasizing the importance of it. This leadership and adherence to the structure will filter down to affect all of the team members and the work displayed and show the ease of the process. If you want your employees to be organized and efficient, you need to lead by example. So, no matter your position, your industry, or even the size of your company, there are several people beyond the project team who are essential to each and every project. They, too, must stay organized and know how everything is systematically arranged.

I remember the first place I worked. The owner had a meeting with me about how important it was to keep the pipeline organized. At first, I did not understand what he was talking about. What is a pipeline? Although I had only worked on smaller projects before and knew what organization meant, I didn't realize that on bigger projects, this organizational structure was called a pipeline.

In this company, the owner was the one creating most of the project folders, which in turn got passed down to the art director and then to everyone else on the team. This model was started with management and flowed all the way down, making unified workflows and processes that made everything run much smoother. And for my first job, it was a good model to follow.

Having a unified structure is also helpful when one of your coworkers is sick or goes on vacation. You don't have to waste time trying to figure out the project structure, making sense of the project and hunting down files; everything is laid out exactly the same so that you can lend a helping hand in any project, if necessary.

Although I keep using the term *projects*, these activities can be anything from project management plans to accounting reports. Regardless of your type of work, you should keep it organized.

If you work for a big production house or an advertising agency with a lot of clients, as an example, chances are you will have many people in and out of projects. I know a couple of companies that like to hire a lot of interns in the summertime. The problem with this is when these interns start working on projects, they tend to be very sloppy, leaving projects in disarray. By strictly enforcing folder structure, it should ensure that your projects will remain organized even after their departure.

If you become the project creator, make sure that you create a good solid folder structure. It is easy to get overwhelmed doing other things and create a project really fast, thinking you will go back and fix it when you have more time. If you were in a hurry to create this project, chances are you will be too busy and forget to fix it. As Hall of Fame basketball player/coach John Wooden states, if you don't have time to do it right the first time, when will you have time to do it over?

CHAPTER SEVEN

TEMPLATING THE PROJECT AND CREATING HARMONY WITH DIRECTORIES

Throughout this book, I have talked about how important it is to stay organized. Once you find what works for you and your business, you need to stick to that consistent format. That's where templating your project comes into play.

As mentioned in previous chapters, you should have a consistent default folder structure. This structure then can be expanded upon, depending on the size and type of your project. You can use this basic default folder structure to template all future projects.

But what is templating? What does that even mean? The definition of template is a mold or pattern, and we use this to define our basic project structure that we will use as a pattern for all future projects. This process is often called templating a project.

But before you commit to a pattern for project templating, test it out. Can we use the structure for multiple projects? Does it work? Does it work *well*? Ask team members for their feedback. They may determine a folder as useless or repetitive, or you may find that they consistently add a particular folder that should be added to the basic structure. Either way, it is always good to discuss this concept with everyone, since they will be the ones working in this folder structure.

It is also important to view the folder structure as it grows and make sure the structure and organization are maintained throughout the project's life cycle. This should be something that the senior developers on the project do, but it never hurts to keep checking on the project.

Once you have the project structure in place, consider the project tools that will help the process move smoothly. As we discussed in Chapter 5, this might include versioning control systems such as Git or SVN to keep everyone connected and pulling the correct resources. These tools should also be built into your project template. I have always liked the old saying "work smarter, not harder," and if you set your projects up right, using both project structure and efficiency tools, you can definitely work smarter.

The project structure and tools are complete, but there is yet another component of templating projects that is critical for organization. Creating a consistent naming convention for your files, folders, and projects are as essential as the project structure itself.

I always teach my programming classes the importance of wording convention when writing code. In the programming world, you can name a lot of things differently, but programmers tend to stay to a strict convention to make it easier when working with a big team. This convention can also be emulated in any digital media area. One example of this would be to name all of your base project files "clientname_projectname," followed by the file extension.

By not using consistent naming conventions, you can make it hard on yourself when you go back to reference old projects or send projects over to the client. I remember when I was told to revise a project that our company had not worked on for over a year. It took me over an hour and a half to find the project because it was not named correctly. It was just named something generic like "Interactive Project 004," with the 004 being the client code. At the time, this made sense to the project manager, but after he left, the number convention left with him. This process included an unnecessary step: all project team members had to look up the client code to find the appropriate client projects. We determined that it would be much easier to include the client's name in the project name so that we would not waste valuable time searching through files in the future.

Again, this naming convention is just one of many naming conventions you can use to incorporate in your project template. You might discover another naming convention that works better for your company and your processes. Whichever naming convention you choose, make sure you relay the information to your team to bring consistency to your projects.

I have mentioned archiving projects. I'm not sure a lot of people think about that, but you really should. Whenever you complete a client's project, that project should be archived and kept for future reference.

From my experience, projects seem to get fractured at this point, because you do not have all of the pieces for the entire project. For a project manager, you have the project structure and all the files you need to successfully complete the project: the audio, video, graphics, and programming files that it took to complete the project, along with any design and development notes needed along the way.

But there are always files that are important to the project that might not be part of this design and development phase; there are always things left out of a project for confidentiality. Project managers may not want developers to see the prices, or they may not want you to see the agreed-upon terms and agreements, but these are all things that should be included in the project when archived. The project manager should archive the project and ensure the project archive includes all details pertaining to the project.

Some people may not agree with this way of archiving projects, but if you only have the project manager archiving and "un"-archiving projects, there should be no reason to worry. This is also helpful if your company grows and more project managers are hired. By keeping these projects organized and structured in the same way, the new project managers can find out everything about a project by un-archiving the projects.

You could also take this manner of archiving one step further and create client folders. Your archived projects will be kept in client folders for even better organization. This sounds very simple, but you wouldn't believe how many people just upload the archived projects onto the server without rhyme or reason.

Once your naming conventions, project structure, and project tools are all in place, it is now time to template all of your projects. By doing this, you create a unified process that makes projects run smoother and more efficiently. But creating harmony between your folders takes time; **don't rush** when creating your project. Do it correctly the first time—you'll save your team a lot of issues later on.

CHAPTER EIGHT

WILL THIS HELP ME GET A JOB? WHAT ELSE?

If you are a student, freelancer, or just working on projects at home, there is nothing better than showing a potential employer your great organization skills. When I would interview potential employees, one of the first things that I looked for was their organizational skills. If you are a programmer, this is definitely one thing a company will look for because it is essential to have good code structure and organization.

I work with a lot of students that are seniors getting ready to graduate and go out and get a job in the industry. Some of them already have jobs, but it astonishes me on how unorganized these students really are. For example, I asked a person to show me the project they were working on. They opened up their computer, revealing over 60 folders on the desktop. It took that student five minutes to find the folder they were trying to show me. If you did this in a job interview, chances are you would not get hired unless you did unbelievable work, and even then, your lack of organization would be a debating factor on whether you were hired or not.

That might sound unbelievable, but out of 20 students I see in my office, over half are that unbelievably unorganized, even after I teach them how to organize their projects. Being organized will only benefit you in getting the job—it will put you ahead of the competition.

Another factor that will help you land a job in your field beyond your job knowledge and skill is understanding the terminology within your industry and within the company.

When you go into an interview, you should sound intelligent and speak intelligently about your industry area. That sounds like a no-brainer, but you would be surprised how many people try to fake it. I had somebody during an interview try to convince me he knew Java, and the whole time he was talking he really meant JavaScript. Java and JavaScript are completely different programming languages. I tried to correct him a couple of times, but he was very adamant that Java was what he was talking about.

He showed me some of his code, and sure enough, it was JavaScript he had been talking about. I showed him some examples and proof that he was indeed talking about JavaScript. In the end, this individual was not hired for the position. This also works in the other direction. Sometimes someone knows what he or she is talking about and can talk very intelligently about the topic, but cannot perform the work. I'm sure you know a person like that, but in this case, they usually get caught when asked to show their projects.

If you are serious about getting a job or changing your career, make sure your projects are structured and organized well and that you are well versed in your industry's terminology. A good way to do this is by following leaders in the industry on Twitter, blogs, or other social media outlets. Being well versed in industry terminology takes time and will consist of a lot of reading, researching, and practicing your skills.

Another way to get leads on employment is to seek out industry user groups in your area and network with people in your field. I cannot say this enough, but networking is one of the best ways to get a job in the media field.

An additional tip I'm sure most of you know (or *should* know) is to not burn your bridges. Be respectful to the company that you're working for if you're going to quit your position. If you can, give them ample notice before you leave. Make sure that you have made all your projects and important files accessible to other employees. When it is your last day, leave everything organized and cleaned up on your desk.

I have been doing freelance work for a few years now, and a lot of the work I get is from former employers. This is because I always left on good terms and gave them ample notice. That is really just being a professional person.

In the end, do good work, be professional, network, and stay organized. You will get the job you want in your field.

CHAPTER NINE

IN THE END

This book, of course, did not demonstrate something cool and fun like creating a 3-D avatar or how to create special effects in a movie, but what I do hope you get out of this is how important it is to create an organized project when you *are* doing cool projects like 3-D avatars and movie special effects. I hope you can take some of these theories and apply them to your career. Good luck!

www.ingramcontent.com/pod-product-compliance
Lightning Source LLC
Chambersburg PA
CBHW052018230326
41598CB00078B/3618